Flying Franks, Floating Fish

The Odd October Skies
of Albuquerque

A loving tribute to photographing twenty years of the Albuquerque
International Balloon Fiesta special shaped balloons

By Kim Alaburda 2006
Flying Franks Publishing
Albuquerque, NM

Featured Hot Air Balloons (*Information gathered from past Albuquerque International Balloon Fiesta programs and at Bart's Special Shape Collection - Olen, Belgiu* bart@specialshapes.nu. *Every effort has been made to note the most appropriate information with the year the photo was taken.*

CONTEST!

You'll notice drawings created by youth throughout the book. These are pictures of special shaped balloons they would like to see. You are invite submit your own drawing (computer generated or hand drawn) for Volume II of *Flying Franks, Floating Fish*. If your drawing is selected for inclusio Volume II . . . you will receive $25 and a complimentary copy of the book! Drawings from *all* ages will be accepted. Send your drawing to Kim Alabu 3909 Juan Tabo Blvd., NE #6, Albuquerque, NM 87111, or your computer generated image to kimalaburda@msn.com by May 30, 2007. You wi notified by September 30, 2007 if your image was selected.

My first hot air balloon sighting occurred while I was driving from Fort Defiance, Arizona to the University of New Mexico in Albuquerque, NM one Monday morning in October of 1981. As I drove on I-40, balloons were flying right over the highway. I nearly crashed at the spectacle.

It wasn't until I moved to Albuquerque in 1985 that I experienced my first Fiesta. Who would think that waking at 5am, usually in absolutely freezing weather (morning temps between 35° - 45°), running through dusty fields (resulting in massive allergy attacks) would prove to be a passion. Go figure.

The first full week of every October is the Albuquerque International Balloon Fiesta. I love running through the field to shoot the newest shape. Or the weirdest. Or the funniest. I love that the pilots and crew talk to you and tell you stories. I love the zebras (field safety) keeping order even when they are loudly suggesting that I slow down. I love running into (very often literally) my fiesta companions whom I typically leave in my dust once we've parked. I love creating my own burrito with chicharrones. I love that after the Special Shapes Rodeo is completed each Thursday and Friday mornings of every Fiesta, and I'm ridiculously exhausted, that I can sit at a bench, eat my burrito and watch as over 600 regular balloons fly INTO the park for the competitions. There is nothing like it. One hand holding the burrito, one hand shooting the balloons as they come right to me. Carne adovada stains aside, it is a perfect moment.

The Fiesta has filled me with hilarious, exciting, stunning, warm experiences. In the Fall of 1985, a friend of mine from Window Rock, Arizona, Loretta Brutz, asked me to visit her sister, Peggy McClanahan, a school teacher from Navajo, NM, who was at St. Joseph's Hospital in downtown Albuquerque being treated for cancer. On one visit in October, she told me that she always wanted to come to see the balloons. She mentioned how ironic it was that she finally got to Albuquerque during the Fiesta, but was laid up in bed too ill to move. I went out into the hall so she wouldn't see me crying like the big baby that I am. I said a really quick, frustrated kind of prayer, something like "would it really kill ya to let her see a few balloons while she's here?!". I went back into her room and, one by one, balloons were flying DIRECTLY in front of her window, landing in the parking lot. It was awesome.

Each Fiesta I shoot well over three hundred photos. Each year, I purchase five copies of the Fiesta program to give to my nieces and nephews. Each year, I also make small balloon books with my photos and give them out to my nieces, nephews and friend's kids. When Betty Caponera and I gave a talk to a class of third graders at St. Gabe's on the southside of Chicago, I was deluged with requests for copies of the cheesy little book I put together. Well, you can see where this is going . . . and here it is — Enjoy!   - Kim Alaburda, September, 2006

All photographs taken by Kim E. Alaburda at the Albuquerque International Balloon Fiestas, 1985 – 2005, Albuquerque, New Mexico.

Sha-moon

3

Space Shuttle
passing up
the moon.

Space Shuttle
hitching a ride
to the moon.

This most excellent balloon was as long as three regular balloons lined up. You would 'Harley' believe it!

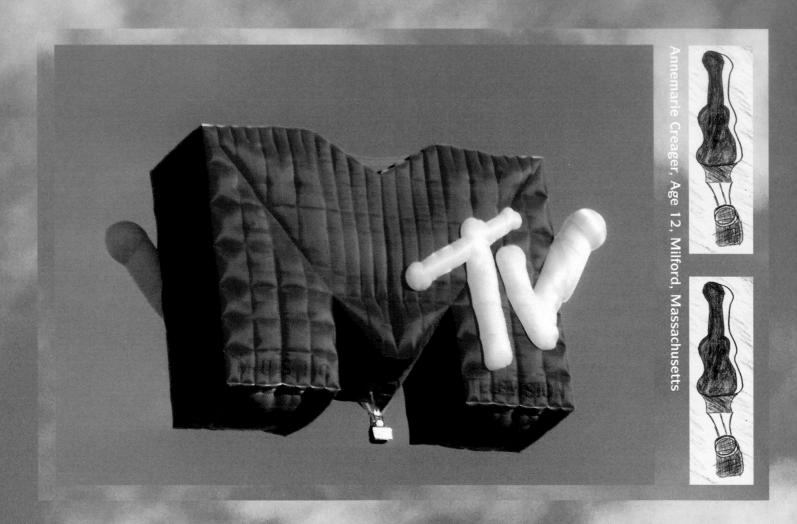

Annemarie Creager, Age 12, Milford, Massachusetts

It's not very often that you get to *see* Music in the air.

Someone said that we all live in this. Must be bigger than it looks.

How funny is this? You're heading to work or school at 8am on a typical Balloon Fiesta day and you see a giant dog. Hot dog. Frank. - flying through the city, over your highway, with mustard. Now that's funny.

It's impossible for me to look at this flying frank and not hear the song 'La Mer' sung by some French guy. (Think Bobby Darrin singing 'Beyond the Sea'). Go get the film 'L.A. Story', by Steve Martin. The opening scene shows a giant frank being flown through the air by a helicopter over Los Angeles while the song is playing. Hilarious.*

* If you're too young, ask a Steve Martin loving relative to get it and then just watch the first five minutes. You'll thank me.

9

Poor, poor little bunny. Fly, bunny, fly!

For the love of God, not Smokey!

I guess if he's mean enough to eat up Smokey, he's mean enough to have his own brother for breakfast. Bad T-Rex, bad.

Uh-oh.

Air-trocities
Giant carnivores nabbing vulnerable prey

. . . That was CLOSE! You turned the page right in the nick of time. Nobody warned me that hot air balloons could be so terrifying.

Good thing it's time for happy, bright, smiling balloons.

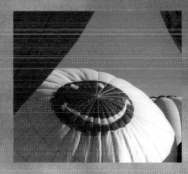

Smiles in the sky – C'mon,
admit it. You smile back.
I know that you do.

"Busy"

Bees

a.k.a., Angelina Duckié

a.k.a., Angelina Fishié

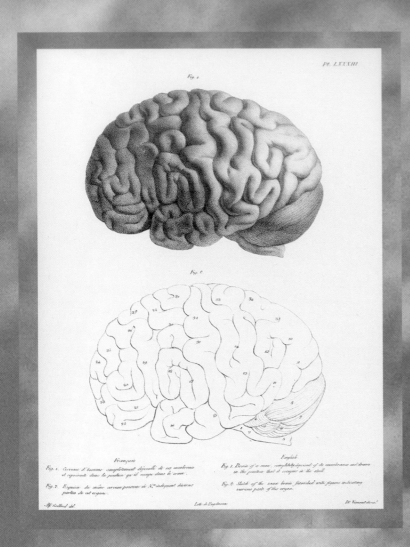

This is your brain.   This is your brain on hot air.

2003

2004

Think somebody's had a little work done? . . . *

* Note the 2003 smile showing
through the 2004 face lift
observable during inflation →

19

Party in the sky.

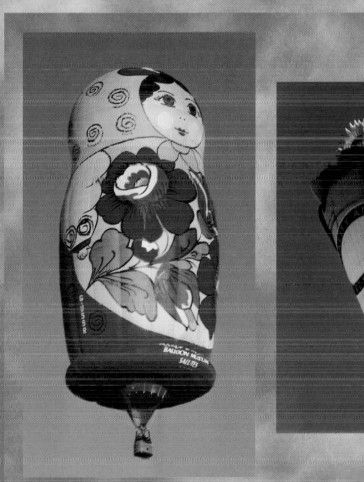

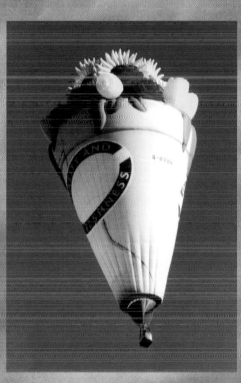

Love is in the air.

High Rise

Living the high life.

♪♪♪♪ "Oh, Canada" ♪♪♪♪

♪♪♪ "Oh, Say Can You See . . . " ♪♪♪

. . . Oh, WOW!

Red Chili Ristra

Zia's

Traditional Symbols of New Mexico

Albuquerque's Enchanted Skies

Happy Humpty.   Not So Happy Humpty.

Real gondola here

October in Albuquerque things get a little topsy turvy.

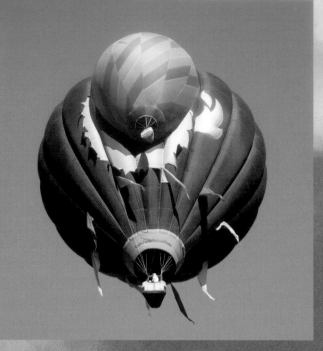

Balloons with things going through them

Air Travel

Elke Heinstein, age 16
Albuquerque, NM

Cars in the sky?
I'm 'wheel'
confused.

Phil Heinstein, Age 17, Albuquerque, NM

Air Traffic

Erick Castillo,
Albuquerque

Air Balls

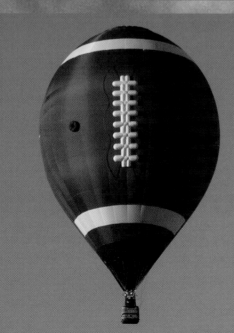

Deana Heinstein, Age 11,
Armstrong, British
Columbia, Canada

Elke Heinstein,
Age 16,
Albuquerque, NM

The only way to fish upon a star.

Wouldn't you love to live in the sky? Me, too.

Bring your kids to the balloon fiesta to get their fruits and vegetables.

Erin Burr, Age 12,
Los Alamos, NM

Sweet Ride

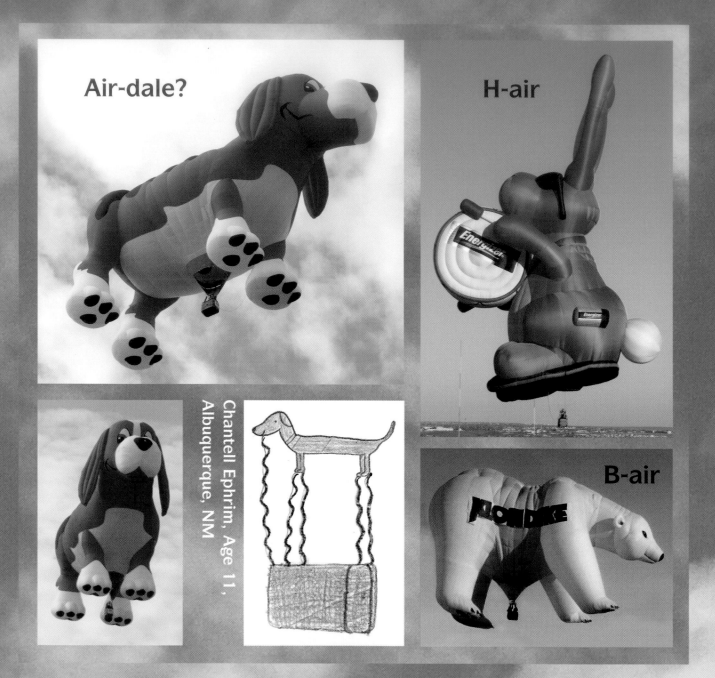

Air-dale?

H-air

B-air

Chantell Ephrim, Age 11,
Albuquerque, NM

Do you know the names of these airborne animals?

Cows in the sky – udder-ly ridiculous!

Youth Gallery
Special Shaped Balloons They'd Like To See

Martin Gubler, Age 13
Kelowna, British
Columbia, Canada

'Christmas'
Steven Calhoun, Age 9
Los Alamos, NM

"Floatin' Around'
Lauren Burr, Age 10,
Los Alamos, NM

Chantell Ephrim,
Age 11,
Albuquerque, NM

'Fishy Sky'
Ally Lakis, Age 5
Los Alamos, NM

'Ducky'
Steven Calhoun, Age 9
Los Alamos, NM

'Batty'
Izzy Lakis, Age 8
Los Alamos, NM

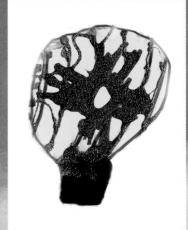

Edwin Perez Fierro,
Age 10
ABQ, NM

Youth Gallery

Special Shaped Balloons They'd Like To See

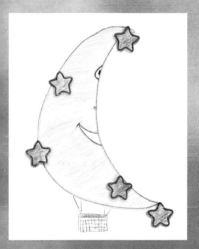

**Elke Heinstein,
Age 16,
ABQ, NM**

**'Tink'
Ciara Gallegos-Ortega,
Age 7, ABQ, NM**

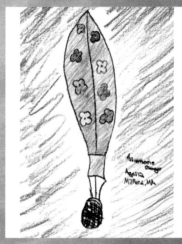

**'Air Surfing'
Annemarie Creager,
Age 12 Milford, MA**

**'The Palm Tree'
Haley Bridgewater,
Age 9 Los Alamos, NM**

**"Crocodile"
Spencer Grebosky,
Age 6. ABQ, NM**

**Jesus Saldaña,
Age 7,
ABQ, NM**

**'Roadrunner Flies'
Stacia Paglieri, Age 9,
White Rock, NM**

**'Milo'
David Heinstein,
Age 13, ABQ, NM**

Dedicated to all my family and friends who humored me with waking at 5am every first week in October in order to get to the field before the balloons started inflating. Then, once we arrived at the Balloon Fiesta Park, they'd watch me and my cameras disappear, madly running from one end of the field to the next (a thousand apologies, zebras). At least we met up for carne adovada and egg burritos!

Annemarie, Mary, Jesse, and Sam Creager
— they always kept up with me!

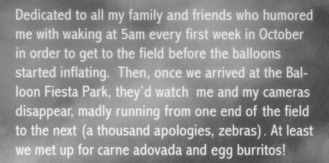

And to Aunt Joan of the Stockyards, a frequent visitor from Canaryville on Chicago's Southside and excellent balloon photographer.

ACKNOWLEDGEMENTS

To my nephew Jake Alaburda who, since he was 2 ½ years old, enthusiastically accompanied me to the Fiesta and to early morning, pajama wearing balloon 'chases'.
You made it so much fun!

To the worldwide creators and owners of the special shaped balloons.

To their pilots who require extreme skill to fly the often anti-aerodynamic shapes.

To Sid Cutter and Tom Rutherford for dreaming up and creating the Albuquerque Balloon Fiesta. I am forever indebted to your huge gamble, personal risk, and wild enthusiasm. (For more info on AIBF: balloonfiesta.com)

To Scott Appelman and Mark Sullivan for creating the Special Shapes Rodeo in 1989. Don't know you, but love you all the same.

To all the staff, volunteers and board of the Albuquerque International Balloon Fiesta — Hugs all around.

To my work staff who so fully supported me during my 'book' sabbatical: Katie Bridgewater, Marcie Davis, Stella Gallegos, Carla Gallegos-Ortega, Ellen Gatewood, and Connie Monahan. This would have NEVER happened without you.

To Cheri Masters for rescuing the book from low resolution hell and providing such a superb camera-ready product just hours before the absolute deadline.

To Sheila Allen, Mary Creager and Rajka Heinstein for constant encouragement, well needed breaks, exceptional tolerance and lamb and bean stew.

To Martin Heinstein and Becky Grebosky for great ideas.

To Betty Caponera for her hilarious and critical edits, many of which I am certain saved me from great personal shame.

Bill, Joanette and Charlie Catino (Chicago), Rajka, David and Philip Heinstein, Betty Caponera, Linda Catino (Chicago)